Charles Darwin

Leslie Buffam

Explore other books at:
WWW.ENGAGEBOOKS.COM

VANCOUVER, B.C.

WWW.ENGAGEBOOKS.COM

Charles Darwin: Level 2
Remarkable People
Leslie Buffam 1949 –
Text © 2023 Engage Books
Design © 2023 Engage Books

Edited by: A.R. Roumanis, Melody Sun,
Ashley Lee & Sarah Harvey
Design by: Mandy Christiansen

Text set in Arial Regular.
Chapter headings set in Fibra One Alt.

FIRST EDITION / FIRST PRINTING

CHARLES DARWIN
NATIONAL PORTRAIT GALLERY
2006

LIBRARY AND ARCHIVES CANADA CATALOGUING IN PUBLICATION

Title: Charles Darwin / Leslie Buffam.
Names: Buffam, Leslie, author.
Description: Series statement: Remarkable people

Identifiers: Canadiana (print) 20230447392 | Canadiana (ebook) 20230447406
ISBN 978-1-77878-308-1 (hardcover)
ISBN 978-1-77878-309-8 (softcover)
ISBN 978-1-77878-310-4 (epub)
ISBN 978-1-77878-311-1 (pdf)
ISBN 978-1-77878-344-9 (audio)

Subjects:
LCSH: Darwin, Charles, 1809-1882—Juvenile literature.
LCSH: Biologists—England— Biography—Juvenile literature.
LCSH: Naturalists—England—Biography—Juvenile literature.
LCSH: Evolution (Biology)—History—Juvenile literature.
LCGFT: Biographies.

Classification: LCC QH31.D2 B83 2023 | DDC J576.8/2092—DC23

This project has been made possible in part
by the Government of Canada.

Canada

Contents

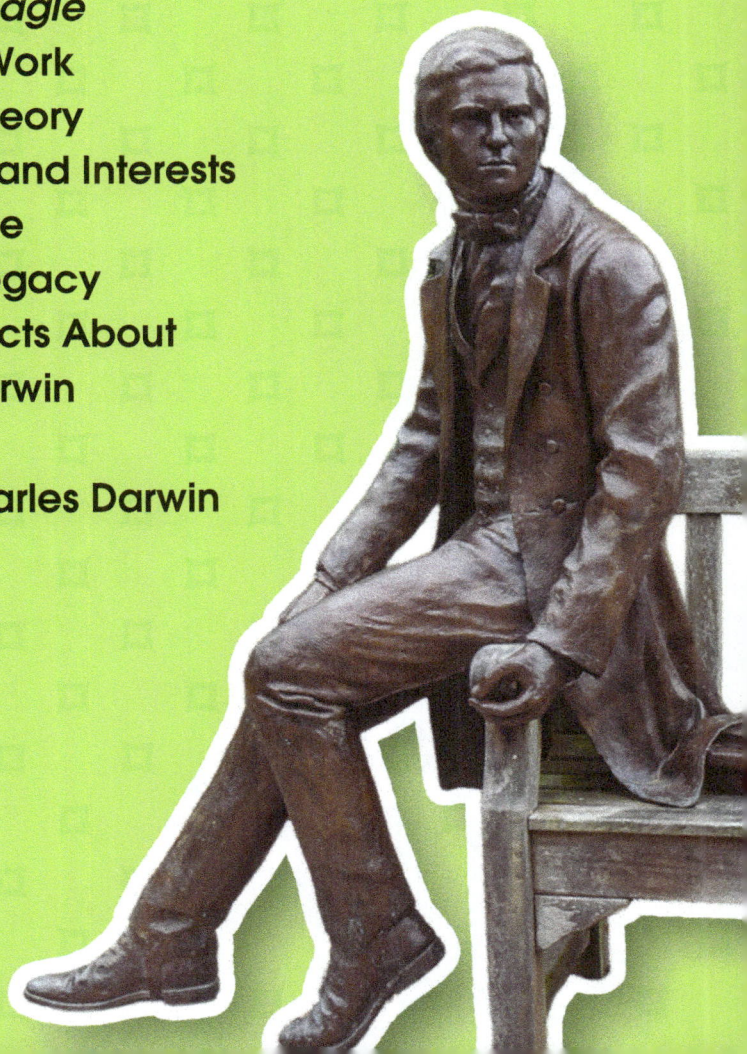

Who Was Charles Darwin?

Charles Robert Darwin was a famous English scientist. Darwin loved studying nature.

Darwin is thought to be one of the greatest scientists ever.

Darwin came up with a **theory** about how plants and animals change over time. It helped people understand why there are so many different kinds of life.

KEY WORD

Theory: an explanation for how or why something in nature works. It is based on ideas that have been tested.

Early Life

Darwin was born on February 12, 1809. His father, Robert, was a doctor. He wanted Charles to be a doctor too.

Robert proved that the eyes move, even when people try to keep them still.

Young Darwin read lots of books about nature. He also liked to explore the land around his home. He collected bugs and plants to study.

British Coleoptera, ex coll. Charles Darwin — Formerly in a cabinet, taken out and left in the present condition by the late G.R. Crotch — See Register, 30.iv.1913

Education

Darwin went to school near his home, but he did not like it. He did not want to study classic books. He wanted to study **natural history**.

KEY WORD
Natural history: the study of living things and other objects in nature.

Darwin's father sent him to medical school in Scotland. Darwin did not like it. He left after two years to go to Christ's College. He could take natural history classes there.

Watching surgery in medical school made Darwin sick.

England During Darwin's Lifetime

English life changed a lot during Darwin's lifetime. **Factories** began to make things that people used to make by hand. Factory owners became rich and powerful.

KEY WORD

Factories: places where machines are used to make things people can buy.

People began moving from the country to cities to work in factories. They thought their lives would be better.

On HMS *Beagle*

In 1831, Darwin got a job as a **naturalist** on a ship called HMS *Beagle*. The ship sailed all around the world.

One of Darwin's jobs was to keep the ship's captain company.

KEY WORD
Naturalist: someone who studies animals and plants.

Darwin wrote a 770-page diary while on HMS *Beagle*.

Darwin's trip around the world took five years. He only spent 18 months on the ship. The rest of his time was spent on land studying nature. He collected samples of different **species**.

KEY WORD

Species: a group of similar animals or plants that can have babies together.

13

Darwin at Work

Darwin returned home in 1836. He began to study all his notes and samples. He had more than 1,500 pages of notes and more than 5,400 animal parts.

CHILIAN EARTH-CREEPER
Upucerthia dumetoria
CHILE
Presented by the Trustees of the British Museum.

Plymouth

Azores

ATLANTIC
OCEAN

Tenerife

PACIFIC
OCEAN

Cape Verde

INDIAN
OCEAN

Cocos (Keeling)

Galapagos

Bahia

Callao - Lima

Mauritius

Valparaiso

Rio de Janeiro

Sydney

Montevideo

King George's
Sound

Hobart

Cape Town

Falkland Islands

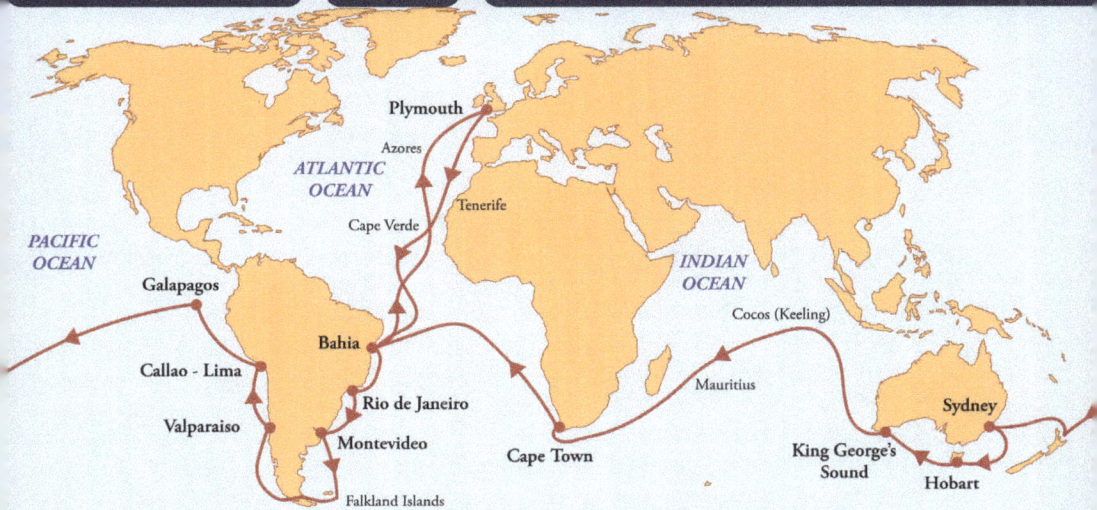

The *Beagle* visited many places including Australia, Africa, and South America.

Darwin turned the diary of his trip into a book in 1839. It was printed many times. The book is called *The Voyage of the Beagle*.

Darwin's Major Work

Darwin believed living things changed over time so they could live better lives. Those that did not change would die. He called this natural selection.

Darwin learned that natural selection caused some birds to have different shaped beaks to be able to eat different foods.

He believed that all life came from a single species. This species changed through natural selection to make new species. This is called the Theory of Evolution by Natural Selection.

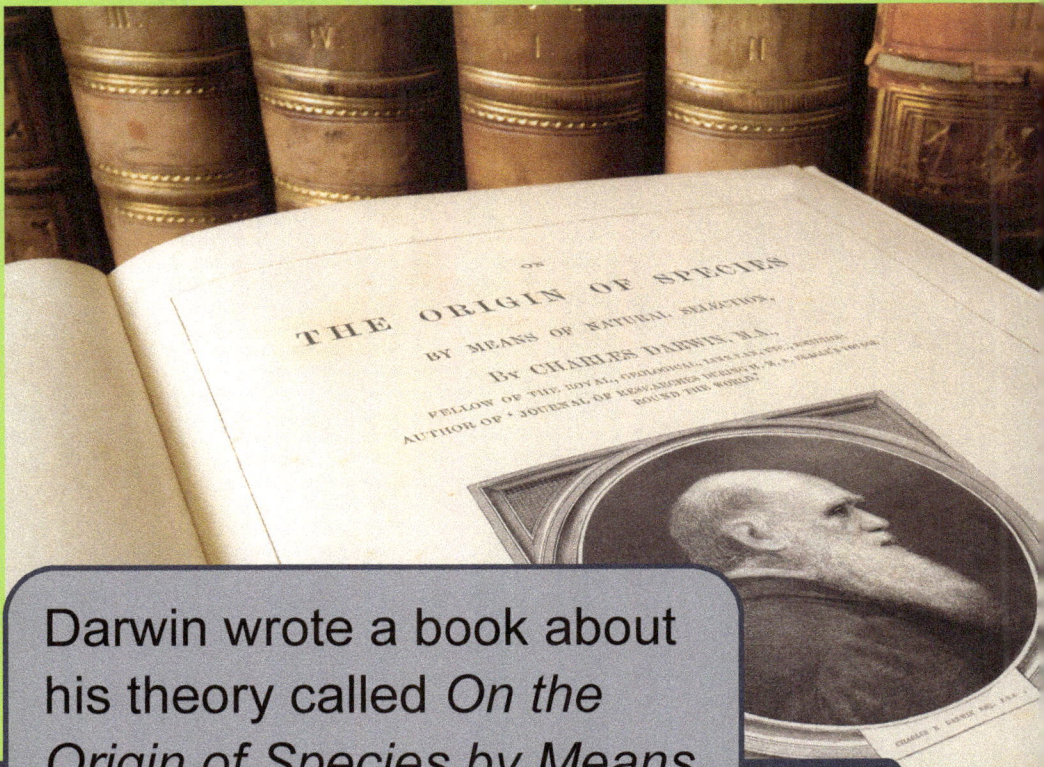

Darwin wrote a book about his theory called *On the Origin of Species by Means of Natural Selection*.

Interests and Influences

Darwin wanted to be like his grandfather, Erasmus. Erasmus was a famous **botanist**. Darwin never met his grandfather, but he read many of his books.

KEY WORD

Botanist: a scientist who studies plants.

Erasmus died before Charles was born.

18

John Henslow was one of Darwin's teachers. He told Darwin to take the job as a naturalist on HMS *Beagle*. This trip is what led Darwin to come up with his theory.

Personal Life

Darwin married Emma Wedgwood in January, 1839. They had ten children together.

Charles and Emma were married for more than forty years. Emma often organized meetings with scientists so Darwin could share his work.

Darwin's Legacy

Darwin's book about his theory made some people angry. They believed God created all living things. Many people believed Darwin's theory and his book became a bestseller.

Some people made drawings and articles that made fun of Darwin and his beliefs.

Darwin's ideas have been **modified** since he wrote them. They are still important to the study of the natural world.

23

KEY WORD
Modified: made small changes in order to make something better.

IT'S TRUE!
Facts About Charles Darwin

Darwin gave his 120 pigeon specimens to the Natural History Museum in 1867.

Darwin was a world expert on barnacles.

Darwin survived an earthquake when he was in South America.

Darwin and Emma played a game called backgammon every night.

One of the first specimens Darwin collected while on HMS *Beagle* was an octopus.

Darwin loved collecting beetles.

TIMELINE

February 12, 1809
Charles Robert Darwin is born

1817
his mother dies

1828
leaves medical school

1828
attends Christ's College

1836
returns to England after traveling the world

1839
writes *The Voyage of the Beagle*

1853
receives Royal Medal for his work on barnacles

1859
On the Origin of Species becomes a bestseller

1818-25 attends public school

1825 is sent to medical school

1831 graduates from Christ's College

1831 gets a job on HMS *Beagle*

January 1839 marries Emma Wedgwood

1842 begins writing down his theory of evolution

April 10, 1882 dies after a heart attack

April 26, 1882 is buried at Westminster Abbey

Be Like Charles Darwin

If you would like to be like Darwin
- Follow your passion in life.
- Take the opportunities given to you.
- Believe in your work.

- Make time for family.
- Work to make your ideas available to all.

- Pay attention to everything around you.

Quiz

Test your knowledge of Charles Darwin by answering the following questions. The questions are based on what you have read in this book. The answers are listed on the bottom of the next page.

1 What did Darwin want to understand?

2 What is a naturalist?

3 What was the name of the ship that began sailing around the world in 1831?

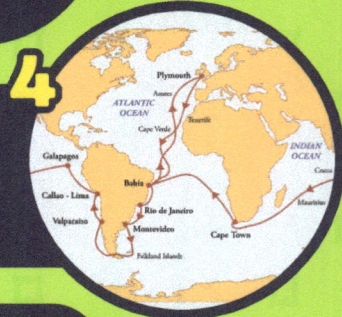

4 When did Darwin turn the diary of his trip into a book?

5 Who did Darwin marry?

6 What was Darwin a world expert on?

Explore other Readers.

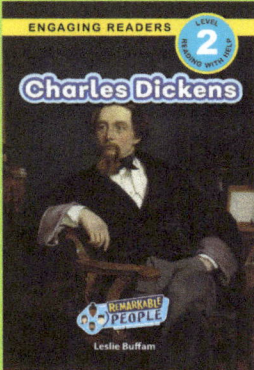

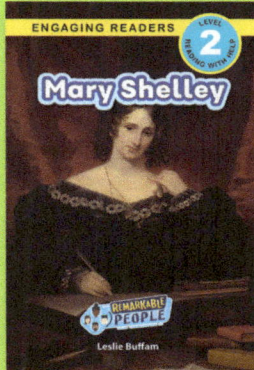

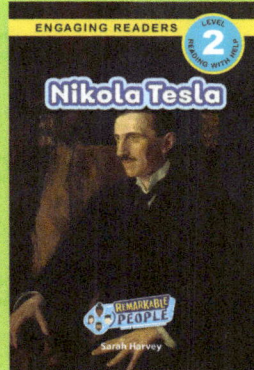

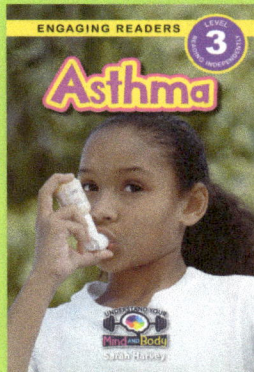

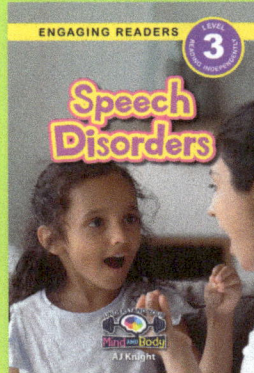

ENGAGING READERS — LEVEL 2
Charles Dickens
REMARKABLE PEOPLE
Leslie Buffam

ENGAGING READERS — LEVEL 2
Mary Shelley
REMARKABLE PEOPLE
Leslie Buffam

ENGAGING READERS — LEVEL 2
Nikola Tesla
REMARKABLE PEOPLE
Sarah Harvey

ENGAGING READERS — LEVEL 3
ADHD
Understand Your Mind and Body
AJ Knight

ENGAGING READERS — LEVEL 3
Asthma
Understand Your Mind and Body
Sarah Harvey

ENGAGING READERS — LEVEL 3
Diabetes
Understand Your Mind and Body
Kit Caudron-Robinson

ENGAGING READERS — LEVEL 3
Obesity
Understand Your Mind and Body
Kit Caudron-Robinson

ENGAGING READERS — LEVEL 3
Speech Disorders
Understand Your Mind and Body
AJ Knight

ENGAGING READERS — LEVEL 3
Vision Loss
Understand Your Mind and Body
Hannalora Leavitt & Sarah Harvey

Visit www.engagebooks.com/readers

Answers: 1. The links between all parts of life 2. Someone who studies animals and plants 3. HMS *Beagle* 4. 1839 5. Emma Wedgwood 6. Barnacles

www.ingramcontent.com/pod-product-compliance
Lightning Source LLC
Chambersburg PA
CBHW051235020426
42331CB00016B/3387